Born to be Wild
Little Polar Bears

Valérie Guidoux

Words that appear in the glossary are printed in
boldface type the first time they occur in the text.

GARETH**STEVENS**
GS
PUBLISHING
A Member of the WRC Media Family of Companies

The Polar Night

During winter in the Far North, the Sun does not rise over the land for weeks. The sky is dark — even at noon. In the Arctic region that circles the North Pole, the Sun is not seen from November through February. During this so-called "polar night," a faint light can barely be seen at noon on the **horizon**. The temperature of the air is about –22° Fahrenheit (–30° Celsius), and the frozen sea forms a huge **ice floe**. This dark, cold, icy place is where polar bears live.

After giving birth to her cubs, a female polar bear stays deep in her **den** and does not care about the icy wind blowing outside. The cubs start life well-sheltered, snuggled tight in their mother's warm fur. They will not come out of the den until they are three months old.

What do you think?

What does a male polar bear do during the winter?

a) It **hibernates** in a den or shelter.

b) It moves south to escape the cold.

c) It hunts for food on the ice floe.

3

During winter, a male polar bear hunts for food on the ice floe.

Polar bears do not hibernate. They stay active all winter because it is the best season for hunting. Only females that are about to have babies take shelter. By October, a female polar bear has finished digging her den and closes herself in. She will not eat again until spring, but her body has enough fat for her to survive and to produce milk to feed her cubs.

A polar bear's den is a cave dug into the snow at the end of a short tunnel. The den's temperature may be freezing cold, but it is much warmer than the air outside.

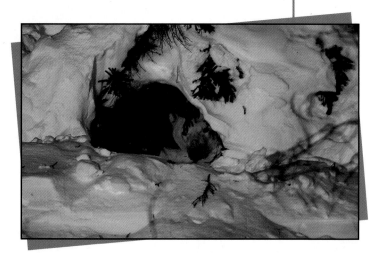

A mother bear's milk is fattening and nutritious. When her cubs leave the den in March or April, they weigh between 20 and 35 pounds (9 and 16 kilograms).

4

A female polar bear usually gives birth to two cubs. The newborn cubs are covered with short hair. They are about 14 inches (35 centimeters) long and weigh a little more than 1 pound (453 grams). Born in December, they spend most of their first three months sleeping, but they wake up to drink their mother's milk and to play. By spring, they have thick fur and follow their mother out into the snow.

A Patient and Skilled Hunter

In April, a low Sun lights up the ice floe, which stretches as far as the eye can see. A little polar bear and its brother slide on a snowdrift, growling like puppies, then fall asleep on their backs and take a short nap. Their mother sits on the ice nearby, watching them out of the corner of her eye. She is quiet and perfectly still, but she never rests. An adult female polar bear is always ready to hunt.

What do you think?

What is a mother polar bear waiting for when she sits quietly on the ice floe?

a) a seal

b) a fish

c) a bird

Polar bears use ice floes to fish in the sea. Under the floes' thick layers of ice, the cold water of the polar seas has some of the richest supplies of food on Earth.

6

A mother polar bear sits quietly, waiting for a seal.

Seals are the main source of food for polar bears during winter. When the sea is covered with ice, seals are easy to catch. When the ice melts, however, they swim much too fast for the bears to chase them underwater.

Many seals live in the polar seas. Seals are **marine mammals**. During winter, they make airholes in the ice floe so they can come up for a breath of air when they are swimming. Polar bears wait for the seals at these breathing holes. When a seal sticks its nose out, the bear catches it with a powerful paw and pulls the seal up onto the ice to eat it.

Sometimes, a polar bear swims under the ice from one airhole to another. Then it will suddenly pop out of the water and grab a seal that is lying on the ice floe.

8

At the beginning of summer, the ice floe begins to break apart, and polar bears can no longer use the breathing holes to hunt seals. Now, they must wait until the seals take naps to catch them. A bear will sneak up on a seal, stopping when the seal looks up. Then, at the last moment, the bear will jump on its **prey**.

Polar bear cubs drink their mothers' milk for at least twenty months. Their survival depends on the success of her seal hunts. If she does not have enough to eat, she will not produce milk, and the cubs will starve to death. More than half of all polar bear cubs die during their first year.

9

Everyone into the Water

During summer in the Arctic, the Sun never seems to set. Even at midnight, its light shines on the horizon, and the day seems to last for months. Huge blocks of ice break off the ice floe and drift through the Arctic Ocean. From May to July, the ice floe melts as the sea flows freely once again. Polar bears spend a lot of time in the water during summer. But, for them, the beginning of the summer season means no seals for dinner.

Resting on a floating block of ice, this little polar bear and its mother do not seem to care where they are going. From time to time, the mother bear dives into the water and eats a fish. Her cub quickly joins her in the water for a swimming lesson — and some fun!

What do you think?

After spending time in the water, how does a polar bear get back to an ice floe?

a) by waiting for the water to freeze again

b) by swimming or by drifting on a block of ice

c) by paddling on a floating log

11

A polar bear gets back to an ice floe by swimming or by drifting on a block of ice.

Even during summer, polar bears never move too far from the water, because the sea is their main source of food. Polar bears are perfectly adapted to water. They often swim for miles (kilometers), but they can also travel long distances by drifting on floating blocks of ice.

A polar bear is protected from the cold by its fur and a thick layer of fat underneath its skin. The bear's fat also helps it float in water.

A polar bear uses its powerful paws to paddle in the water. Its fingers are linked together with skin to form a large flipper. Polar bears can swim a long distance without stopping.

12

When it comes out of the water, a polar bear shakes itself like a dog. Underneath its long waterproof hair, the bear has very **dense** fur that keeps its skin dry.

A mother bear cleans her coat after each meal by licking it, rubbing herself in the snow, or jumping into the water. She teaches her cubs how to clean themselves, too, because dirty hair will not protect them from the cold as well as clean hair.

13

A Fur Coat Is No Fun in Summer

On a snowy beach, young polar bears run here and there. They have fun making geese fly away. Far behind them, the mother bear walks slowly. She is hot in her heavy fur coat and does not even try to catch a bird. Adult bears do not become excited over such small prey. In the summer heat, a mother bear prefers diving into the cold sea or lying down in the hollow of a cool rock while she waits for her active cubs to quiet down.

What do you think?

What color is the hair of a polar bear's coat?

a) white

b) white and yellow

c) clear

If humans ran around wearing heavy coats, they would get very hot very fast. With its thick fur coat, an adult polar bear never runs for very long. A young bear, however, does not have as much fur, so it can run a long distance before it becomes too hot.

The hair of a polar bear's coat is clear.

Although it looks white, a polar bear's hair is clear, and each hair has a hollow center. Sunlight bounces off the hair and makes the bear look white. The clear, hollow hair allows sunlight to reach the bear's black skin, which soaks up the Sun's heat.

Once this heat is trapped, it does not leave the bear's body because the bear's fur is so dense. In winter, its fur keeps a polar bear warm, but in summer, the bear can become very hot!

Polar bears are less active in summer than in winter. During warm weather, they take many naps. To cool off, they look for snowdrifts on which they can sleep, or they dig holes in the ground.

16

Even during winter, a polar bear does not run for a long time because it becomes hot very quickly.

During summer, polar bears have a hard time hunting. They avoid running but will swim to catch fish and capture **seabirds** resting on the water.

Between activities, a bear lies tummy up. Its fur is less dense on the underside of its body so lying in this position helps the bear release some of its body heat to cool off.

17

On the Move

The **Inuit** name for polar bears means "the wandering." The Inuit are the Native people who live in the Arctic. All summer long, little polar bears and their mothers wander throughout the Far North in search of food. Sometimes, the food they find smells very bad, such as a dead animal on the shore. A dead, **beached** whale might attract a dozen male bears, and they all share in eating it. Although she is hungry, a mother bear will stay away from the feast. Because she does not trust the male bears, she will eat later.

As soon as ice forms, in about the middle of October, polar bears venture onto the ice floe. During the coming winter, mother polar bears will teach their cubs how to hunt seals. Polar bear cubs stay with their mothers until they are two years old.

What do you think?

Why doesn't a mother polar bear trust male polar bears?

a) because the male bears do not share their food

b) because the male bears might eat her little cubs

c) because male bears fight with female bears

19

A mother bear does not trust male bears because they might eat her cubs.

A female bear comes near a male bear only in the spring, when polar bears **mate**. She takes care of her babies by herself, carefully protects them, and never lets a male near them. Several mother bears will sometimes gather, however, and their cubs will play together.

Every fall, several polar bears come to eat at the garbage dump in Churchill, a Canadian city on Hudson Bay.

20

At the beginning of its third winter, a young polar bear will leave its mother. It will travel about 600 miles (965 km) to find a huge **territory** of its own. After choosing its territory, the bear will explore all parts of this area every year.

Polar bears are very comfortable on ice. They have rough pads on the bottoms of their paws that stop them from sliding.

21

Polar bears are mammals. They are also carnivores, which means they eat mainly meat. Polar bears are found in Alaska, Canada, Greenland, and Russia, living on ice floes and along the Arctic coast that surrounds the North Pole. An adult male polar bear can weigh from 775 to 1,500 pounds (350 to 680 kg), or more. A female weighs between 330 and 550 pounds (150 and 250 kg). In the wild, polar bears live about fifteen years. In captivity, they can live twenty-five to thirty years.

Polar bears are related to other bears, including brown bears, grizzlies, and giant pandas.

A polar bear has small ears so that it does not lose any heat through them.

A polar bear has an excellent sense of smell. When it hunts, the bear's nose helps it find seals' breathing holes.

Its strong, 2-inch (5-cm) claws are dangerous weapons.

Like other carnivores, polar bears have very sharp teeth — long, pointed front teeth to seize prey and sharp back teeth to tear the meat.

Polar bears can run 25 miles (40 km) per hour — almost as fast as a car on a city street.

A polar bear is about 8 feet (244 centimeters) long and about 5 feet (152 cm) high from the ground to the top of its shoulders.

The spaces between polar bears' toes are webbed to help them swim.

A polar bear's paws are very large. They help spread out the bear's weight so the animal will not sink into the snow and can walk on thin ice without breaking it.

23

GLOSSARY

beached — driven or washed up onto a shore and unable to move back into the water

den — a cave or hollow that a wild animal uses for shelter

dense — having parts that are packed closely together

hibernates — spends the winter in an inactive state, such as sleeping or resting

horizon — the line in the distance along which the earth and the sky seem to meet

ice floe — a large, flat area of ice floating in a body of water

Inuit — the Native people who live in the Arctic regions of North America and Russia

mammals — warm-blooded animals that have backbones, give birth to live babies, feed their young with milk from the mother's body, and have skin that is usually covered with hair or fur

marine — of, related to, or living in the sea

mate — (v) to join together to produce young

prey — animals that are hunted and killed by other animals

seabirds — birds that spend a lot of time on the open ocean

territory — an area of land that an animal occupies and defends

venture — to take on the risks and dangers of an activity

Please visit our web site at: www.garethstevens.com
For a free color catalog describing Gareth Stevens Publishing's list of high-quality books and multimedia programs, call 1-800-542-2595 (USA) or 1-800-387-3178 (Canada). Gareth Stevens Publishing's fax: (414) 332-3567.

Library of Congress Cataloging-in-Publication Data

Guidoux, Valérie.
    [Petit ours blanc. English]
    Little polar bears / Valérie Guidoux. — North American ed.
        p. cm. — (Born to be wild)
    ISBN 0-8368-4739-3 (lib. bdg.)
    1. Polar Bear—Infancy—Juvenile literature. I. Title. II. Series.
QL737.C27G8513   2005
599.786'139—dc22   2004065366

This North American edition first published in 2006 by
Gareth Stevens Publishing
A Member of the WRC Media Family of Companies
330 West Olive Street, Suite 100
Milwaukee, Wisconsin 53212 USA

First published in 2003 as *Le petit ours blanc* by Mango Jeunesse, an imprint of Editions Mango, Paris, France.
Picture Credits (t=top, b=bottom, l=left, r=right)
Bios: C. Ruoso 13(br), 20, 21(t); F. Berndt 7; K. Wothe 13(tl); V. Fournier 15; R. Valarcher 18. Colibri: Ch. Simon title page, back cover, 12(tr), 22; Negro-Crétu 5; B&C Baranger 8(both), 12(b); C. Balcœur 9(both); Pouyfourcat 17(all). Sunset: S. T. F cover; G. Lacz 2, 4(both), 10, 23; C. Simon 16; B. Simon 21(b).

English translation: Muriel Castille
Gareth Stevens editor: Barbara Kiely Miller
Gareth Stevens art direction: Tammy West
Gareth Stevens designer: Jenni Gaylord

Printed in the United States of America

1 2 3 4 5 6 7 8 9 09 08 07 06 05